博古通今学汉语丛书

Gems of the Chinese Language Through the Ages

名句 101

101 Chinese Quotes

蔡希勤　编著
韩芙芸　翻译

SinolinguA
华语教学出版社

First Edition 2017

Third Printing 2024

ISBN 978-7-5138-1328-0

Published by Sinolingua Co., Ltd

24 Baiwanzhuang Street, Beijing 100037, China

Tel: (86) 10-68320585 68997826

Fax: (86) 10-68997826 68326333

http://www.sinolingua.com.cn

E-mail: hyjx@sinolingua.com.cn

Printed by Beijing Hucais Culture Communication Co., Ltd

Printed in the People's Republic of China

前　言

学习汉语的外国学生，当他们初步掌握了汉语的语音、词汇、语法和文字时，很想进一步提高自己的汉语水平。怎样提高呢？一件重要的事就是需要掌握一些汉语语言中最有特色的东西，例如成语、谚语、歇后语、典故、名句和惯用语。这些东西既和汉语汉字有密切关系，又和中华民族的文化背景有密切关系。掌握了它们，不但能够丰富外国人汉语的表达能力，而且也能够增强他们汉语表达的本土特色。简而言之，他们所掌握的汉语就更像汉语了。这就向成为一个“中国通”迈出了重要的一步。

为以上目的，我们给这样的外国学生编了一套“博古通今学汉语丛书”，包括“成语101”“谚语 101”“歇后语 101”“典故 101”“名句 101”和“惯用语 101”。

本套书精选汉语中最有价值的、常用的、表现力强的成语、谚语、歇后语、典故、名句和惯用语各 101 则。每则均附英文释义，并配一幅精美插图，另对一些难解词语给出中英文注释。

Preface

What comes next for the student of Chinese as a second language after mastering its phonetics, grammar, and most of its vocabulary? The next highly desirable step would be to study some of the more typical Chinese expressions, such as its idioms and set phrases, two-part allegorical sayings, allusions, famous quotes or even colloquial Chinese phrases. These expressions are so closely related to the Chinese language and culture that once one has mastered them, one will not only be able to speak idiomatic Chinese and sound more like a native speaker, but will also be able to penetrate deeper into Chinese culture and gradually become a "China Hand."

For this purpose, we have compiled this series—Gems of the Chinese Language Through the Ages which comprises the following six titles:

101 Common Chinese Idioms and Set Phrases

101 Pearls of Chinese Wisdom

101 Chinese Two-Part Allegorical Sayings

The Stories Behind 101 Chinese Idioms

101 Chinese Quotes

101 Modern Chinese Phrases

These idioms and sayings have been chosen for the frequency with which they are used, their practical value and their expressiveness. Each is accompanied by an English translation and an illustration. Some of the more obscure expressions have been further annotated in both Chinese and English.

目 录

Contents

名句 101

101 Chinese Quotes

1. Shuí yán cùn cǎo xīn,
谁言寸草心，

bào dé sān chūn huī.
报得三春晖。

Such kindness as the young grass receives,
the warm sun can't be repaid.

—translated by Xu Yuanchong

出处 Source:

慈母手中线，游子身上衣。临行密密缝，意恐迟迟归。谁言寸草心，报得三春晖。

——唐·孟郊《游子吟》

注释 Notes:

寸草：小草，比喻儿女。春晖：春天的阳光，比喻父母对儿女的慈爱抚养。谁能说儿女像小草一样的那点孝心，可以报答慈母春晖般的恩惠。比喻儿女对父母养育之恩的无限感激之情。

寸草（cùn cǎo），young grass, is a metaphor for sons and daughters; while 春晖（chūn huī），the spring sunshine, refers to the care and affection from parents. Filial piety is ingrained in Chinese culture. It is believed that the gratitude from young grass (children) can hardly repay the loving care from the spring sunshine (parents). These lines express children's profound gratitude toward their parents.

应用 Example sentences:

甲：儿女对父母的养育之恩是永远报答不完的。

乙：是啊！谁言寸草心，报得三春晖。

Lǎo jì fú lì , zhì zài qiān lǐ ;
2. 老骥伏枥，志在千里；
lièshì mùnián , zhuàng xīn bù yǐ .
烈士暮年，壮心不已。

Just like an old steed in the stable still aspires to gallop a thousand miles, an aged hero still possesses high aspirations.

出处 Source:

神龟虽寿，犹有竟时；螣蛇乘雾，终为土灰。老骥伏枥，志在千里；烈士暮年，壮心不已。盈缩之期，不但在天；养怡之福，可得永年。幸甚至哉，歌以咏志。

——东汉·曹操《步出夏门行·龟虽寿》

注释 Notes:

骥：好马，千里马。枥：马槽。烈士：指有志于建立功业的人。千里马虽老，仍想着奔驰千里疆场；豪杰之士虽已年老，建功立业的雄心犹壮。

骥（jì）means warhorse. 枥（lì）means stable. 烈士（lièshì）refers to a person who is ambitious and wants to make outstanding achievements.

应用 Example sentences:

甲：老科学家在病房里，想着那未竟的事业止不住地叹气。

乙：真是“老骥伏枥，志在千里；烈士暮年，壮心不已”。

Lián zhě , zhèng zhī běn yě ;
3. 廉者，政之本也；
ràng zhě , dé zhī zhǔ yě .
让者，德之主也。

Incorruption forms the fundamentals of politics. Humility molds the basis of morality.

出处 Source:

且婴闻之，廉者，政之本也；让者，德之主也。栾高不让，以至此祸，可毋慎乎！廉之谓公正，让之谓保德。

——春秋·晏婴《晏子春秋·内篇杂下》

注释 Notes:

本，根本。主，主要的东西。政治的根本是廉洁，道德的根基是谦让。

本（běn）：basis, foundation. 主（zhǔ）：key content.

应用 Example sentences:

甲：现在有的官员贪得无厌，利用权力进行不正当交易。

乙：“廉者，政之本也”，一定要把这些贪婪的坏人清理出去。

Bó guān ér yuē qǔ , hòu jī ér bó fā .

4. 博观而约取，厚积而薄发。

Absorb the best knowledge after extensive reading, express one's opinion concisely on the basis of rich growth.

出处 Source:

博观而约取，厚积而薄发，吾告子止于此矣。

——宋·苏轼《杂说·送张琥》

注释 Notes:

博观：博览群书。约取：吸取精华。厚积：学问累积丰富。薄发:（知识学问）慢慢地放出。做学问要博览群书汲取精华，广积知识简约表达。

博观（bó guān）means to read widely. 约取（yuē qǔ）means to absorb the best from the books. 厚积（hòu jī）means to accumulate rich knowledge. 薄发（bó fā）means to give comment concisely.

应用 Example sentences:

甲：老师，做学问的正确方法是什么？

乙：做学问要“博观而约取，厚积而薄发”，切忌一知半解。

Bù jī kuǐ bù , wú yǐ zhì qiān lǐ ;
5. 不积跬步，无以至千里；
bù jī xiǎo liú , wú yǐ chéng jiāng hǎi .
不积小流，无以成 江海。

A journey of one thousand miles is completed by every step on the way; an ocean or a river is formed by the inflow of every brook and stream.

出处 Source:

不积跬步，无以至千里；不积小流，无以成江海。骐骥一跃，不能十步；驽马十驾，功在不舍。

——战国·荀况《荀子·劝学》

注释 Notes:

跬步：半步。古代的半步相当于现在的一步。这句话的意思是说不一步一步走，就到不了千里之远；不汇聚一条条细流，就成不了江海。比喻做学问要靠日积月累才能成功。

跬步（kuǐ bù）means half a step in ancient times which is equivalent to one full step nowadays. This sentence means that rich knowledge can only be acquired by accumulation over an extended period.

应用 Example sentences:

甲：老师，中国文化博大精深，我该怎么去学习才能成功呢？

乙：不积跬步，无以至千里；不积小流，无以成江海。你不要一味图快，只要不断努力，就能成功。

Bù shí Lú Shān zhēn miànmù ,
6. 不识庐山真面目，
zhǐ yuán shēn zài cǐ shān zhōng .
只缘身在此山中。

I see not the true face of Mount Lushan as I am right in it.

出处 Source:

横看成岭侧成峰，远近高低各不同。不识庐山真面目，只缘身在此山中。

——宋·苏轼《题西林壁》

注释 Notes:

缘：因为。苏轼游庐山，在山中通过横看、侧看、远看、近看，发现景色各不相同。由此他认识到，因为自己置身于山中（局部），反而看不清庐山全貌（真面目）。后常用这句话比喻当局者迷，旁观者清。

缘（yuán）：because. These sentences are from a poem by Su Shi (1037-1101) composed when he visited Mount Lushan. In the mountain, he wrote, "The scenery varies when people watch from close or afar, or from different sides." Mount Lushan will not show its true features just because people are right in the mountain. It is used nowadays to mean that those closely involved cannot see the situation clearly.

应用 Example sentences:

甲：我们天天在一起工作，我怎么会不了解他呢？

乙：这正是"不识庐山真面目，只缘身在此山中"了。

Xīyáng wúxiàn hǎo, zhǐ shì jìn huánghūn.

7. 夕阳无限好，只是近黄昏。

The setting sun seems so sublime, but it is near its dying time.

—translated by Xu Yuanchong

出处 Source:

向晚意不适，驱车登古原。夕阳无限好，只是近黄昏。

——唐·李商隐《登乐游原》

注释 Notes:

无限壮美的夕阳晚景虽好，却已经接近黄昏时分。

The lines, especially the first line, are often quoted to refer to advanced age.

应用 Example sentences:

甲：她演了一辈子配角，想不到晚年却大放异彩。

乙：可惜“夕阳无限好，只是近黄昏”。

Bù yǐ guīju , bù néng chéng fāngyuán .

8. 不以规矩，不能成方圆。

Without a compass and a ruler, one cannot form squares and circles.

出处 Source:

离娄之明，公输子之巧，不以规矩，不能成方圆。

——战国·孟轲《孟子·离娄上》

注释 Notes:

规：圆规。矩：曲尺。没有规矩，做不出方形和圆形的东西。比喻做事要遵循一定的法则。

规（guī）：compass. 矩（jǔ）：L-shaped ruler. This quote is a metaphor used to illustrate how rules and regulations must be adhered to in handling affairs.

应用 Example sentences：

甲：当上总经理的第一天，我先给下属订立了一套工作制度。

乙：有道理，“不以规矩，无以成方圆”啊。

Bú yì ér fù qiě guì , yú wǒ rú fúyún .

9. 不义而富且贵，于我如浮云。

Ill-gotten wealth and rank are just like fleeting clouds to me.

出处 Source:

子曰:“饭疏食饮水,曲肱而枕之,乐亦在其中矣。不义而富且贵,于我如浮云。”

——春秋·孔丘《论语·述而》

注释 Notes:

用不正当手段得来的富贵,对我来说就像浮云一样,(我不会去选择)。

This quote is from *The Analects*. It shows Confucianism denounces wealth and rank pursued in dishonest ways.

应用 Example sentences:

甲:很多人升官发财了,你何必如此清苦?

乙:“不义而富且贵,于我如浮云”,我是不会同流合污的。

Bú zhàn ér qū rén zhī bīng , shàn zhī shàn
10. 不战而屈人之兵，善之善
zhě yě .
者也。

The supreme art of war is to break the enemy's resistance without fighting.

出处 Source:

百战百胜，非善之善者也，不战而屈人之兵，善之善者也。

——春秋 · 孙武《孙子兵法 · 谋攻》

注释 Notes:

屈：使屈服。不经交战就能使敌人屈服，才是最好的谋略。

屈（qū）：to subdue.

应用 Example sentences:

甲：你说百战百胜还不算最好的谋略吗？

乙：是的，“不战而屈人之兵”才是最好的谋略。

Chā yǐ háolí , miù yǐ qiān lǐ .

11. 差以毫厘，谬以千里。

A minimal error may lead you a thousand miles astray.

出处 Source:

故《易》曰：“差以毫厘，谬以千里。”

——东汉·班固《汉书·司马迁传》

注释 Notes:

毫厘：极短的长度。谬：差错。形容极细微的差错，会造成严重的后果。

毫厘（háolí）：a very short length. 谬（miù）：error. This phrase is used to describe how a minor mistake may result in serious consequences.

应用 Example sentences:

甲：整理古籍要格外严肃认真，一点差错不能出。

乙：是的，否则“差以毫厘，谬以千里”，后果就严重了。

Chī yí qiàn , zhǎng yí zhì .

12. 吃一堑，长一智。

A fall into the pit, a gain in your wit.

出处 Source:

经一蹶者长一智，今日之失，未必不为后日之得。

——明·王守仁《与薛尚谦书》

注释 Notes:

堑：壕沟，比喻困难、挫折。智：智慧，见识。受到一次挫折，便得到一次教训，增长一分才智。

堑（qiàn）：ditch or setback. 智（zhì）：wit, wisdom or knowledge. Wit is gained from each mistake or setback.

应用 Example sentences:

甲：吃了一次亏，就要长一次记性。

乙：是，“吃一堑，长一智”嘛！

Dé dào zhě duō zhù, shī dào zhě guǎ zhù.

13. 得道者多助，失道者寡助。

A just cause enjoys abundant support; an unjust cause finds little support.

出处 Source:

得道者多助，失道者寡助。寡助之至，亲戚畔之；多助之至，天下顺之。

——战国·孟轲《孟子·公孙丑下》

注释 Notes:

道：正义。坚持正义的人会得到多方面的支持与帮助，违背正义的人必然陷于孤立。

道（dào）：justice.

应用 Example sentences:

甲：因为他主持正义，大家都团结在他的周围。

乙：这就是得道者多助，失道者寡助。

Dú shū bǎi biàn, qí yì zì xiàn.

14. 读书百遍，其义自见。

When a book is read a hundred times, its meanings will naturally become clear.

出处 Source:

（董）遇善治《老子》，为《老子》作训注；又善《左氏传》……人有从学者，遇不肯教，云："必当先读百遍。"言"读书百遍，其义自见。"

——三国·鱼豢《魏略》

注释 Notes:

见：同"现"，显露。能把一本书读过百遍，其中的含义自然就会显现出来。

见（xiàn）：become clear, become evident

应用 Example sentences:

甲：老师，这篇古文我读了几遍，还是不太明白。

乙：古人说"读书百遍，其义自见"，你应该再多读几遍。

Chǐ yǒu suǒ duǎn, cùn yǒu suǒ cháng.

15. 尺有所短，寸有所长。

A foot may prove short while an inch may prove long.

出处 Source:

夫尺有所短，寸有所长；物有所不足，智有所不明。

——战国·屈原《卜居》

注释 Notes:

尺虽比寸长，但和更长的东西相比，就显得短；寸虽比尺短，但和更短的东西相比，就显得长。比喻人或事物各有短处，也各有长处，不能一概而论。

A foot is longer than an inch, but it is surely shorter than other longer objects; an inch is shorter than a foot, but it is surely longer than something shorter. This quote is a metaphor used to show every person or object has strong and weak points.

应用 Example sentences:

甲：这次比赛，想不到他会输给一个名不见经传的新人。

乙：这就叫“尺有所短，寸有所长”。

Chū yūní ér bù rǎn ,
16. 出淤泥而不染，
zhuó qīng lián ér bù yāo .
濯清涟而不妖。

The lotus flower grows in mud, yet is never contaminated by it. It floats on waving water, yet never dances with it.

出处 Source:

自李唐来，世人盛爱牡丹。予独爱莲之出淤泥而不染，濯清涟而不妖，中通外直，不蔓不枝，香远益清，亭亭净植，可远观而不可亵玩焉！

——宋·周敦颐《爱莲说》

注释 Notes:

濯：洗涤。清涟：清澈的水。妖：艳丽而轻薄。莲花生于淤泥中而不受污染，长在清水中而不妖冶。比喻正直的人不为世俗所污，能保持高贵的品德。

濯（zhuó）: to wash. 清涟（qīng lián）: clear water. 妖（yāo）: flirtatious. This phrase means an upright person will keep their integrity uncontaminated by earthly vices.

应用 Example sentences:

甲：她虽然出生在大汉奸家庭，却保持着一个革命者的节操。

乙：真是“出淤泥而不染”呀！

Chūncán dào sǐ sī fāng jìn ,
17. 春蚕到死丝方尽，
làjù chéng huī lèi shǐ gān .
蜡炬成灰泪始干。

A spring silkworm spins silk until its death; candles only when burned up have no tears to shed.

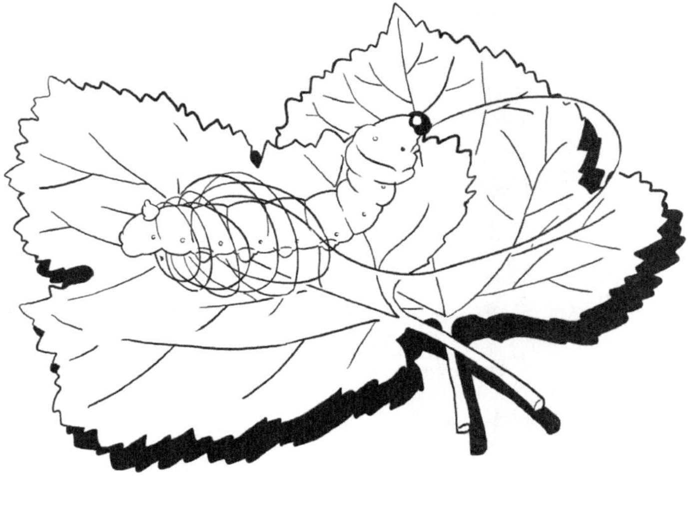

出处 Source:

相见时难别亦难，东风无力百花残。春蚕到死丝方尽，蜡炬成灰泪始干。

——唐·李商隐《无题》

注释 Notes:

丝：双关语，与“思”相谐。相逢难，离别更难，百花已随东风凋谢。只有思念像春蚕吐丝，至死方休；像蜡烛照明，直到成灰泪才流干。比喻对爱情始终如一，或对事业坚持不懈。

丝（sī）：silk, a homophone for missing someone. This phrase is used to describe a persistent attitude toward love or a cause.

应用 Example sentences:

甲：他日夜思念远方的爱人，已经到了茶不思饭不想的地步。

乙：这真是“春蚕到死丝方尽，蜡炬成灰泪始干”呀！

Dàn yuàn rén chángjiǔ , qiān lǐ gòng chánjuān .

18. 但愿人长久，千里共婵娟。

Let us wish that a man may live as long as he can. Though miles apart, we'll share the beauty the moon displays.

—translated by Xu Yuanchong

出处 Source:

明月几时有？把酒问青天。不知天上宫阙，今夕是何年。我欲乘风归去，又恐琼楼玉宇，高处不胜寒。起舞弄清影，何似在人间！

转朱阁，低绮户，照无眠。不应有恨，何事长向别时圆？人有悲欢离合，月有阴晴圆缺，此事古难全。但愿人长久，千里共婵娟。

——宋·苏轼《水调歌头》

注释 Notes:

婵娟：本指美好的姿色，此处代指月色。只愿千里之外的亲人身体健康，和我共赏这明媚皎洁的月色。

婵娟（chánjuān）originally means charming elegance. Here it refers to moonlight. This quote is often used to wish for the good health of one's family who lives somewhere else.

应用 Example sentences:

甲：看到天上的一轮明月，我就会思念千里之外的亲人。

乙：但愿人长久，千里共婵娟。

Dāng duàn bú duàn, fǎn shòu qí luàn.

19. 当断不断，反受其乱。

Indecision invariably leads to trouble.

出处 Source:

（齐相）召平曰："嗟乎！道家之言'当断不断，反受其乱'乃是也。"

——西汉·司马迁《史记·齐悼惠王世家》

注释 Notes:

断：决断。受：遭受。乱：祸。意思是应当做出决断时而不决断，最后反而给自己招来祸害。

断（duàn）: be decisive. 受（shòu）: to suffer. 乱（luàn）: trouble.

应用 Example sentences:

甲：我后悔当初没有开除他，结果今天他给公司惹这么大的麻烦。

乙：这就叫"当断不断，反受其乱"。

Dāng jú zhě mí , páng guān zhě qīng .

20. 当局者迷，旁观者清。

Those closely involved cannot see clearly, while the onlookers see most of the game.

出处 Source:

当局者迷，旁观必审。（审：清楚地知道。后多作“旁观者清”。）

——北宋·宋祁等《新唐书·元行冲传》

注释 Notes:

当局者，原指下棋的人。旁观者，原指看人下棋的人。比喻当事人往往因对利害得失考虑过多而陷于主观片面，反而不及局外人看得全面、客观。

当局者（dāng jú zhě）originally meant those who play chess. 旁观者（páng guān zhě）meant bystanders who watch a chess match. The sentence means an outsider sees more objectively than the person whose interests are bound up in the matter.

应用 Example sentences:

甲：开一天会也没有弄明白怎么回事。

乙：可见“当局者迷，旁观者清”。

Dú shū pò wàn juǎn , xiàbǐ rú yǒu shén .

21. 读书破万卷，下笔如有神。

Having read more than ten thousand books, one will surely own a gifted pen.

出处 Source:

甫昔少年日，早充观国宾；读书破万卷，下笔如有神。赋料扬雄敌，诗看子建亲；李邕求识面，王翰愿卜邻。

——唐·杜甫《奉赠韦左丞丈二十二韵》

注释 Notes:

读书读得多了，下笔写文章就如有神助。

Read more books and you will write more fluently.

应用 Example sentences:

甲：老师，我每次写作文搜肠刮肚也想不出词儿来。

乙：古人说“读书破万卷，下笔如有神”，你还要多多阅读。

Duō xíng búyì bì zì bì .

22. 多行不义必自毙。

Frequent evil deeds will bring ruin to the doer.

出处 Source:

蔡仲曰："姜氏何厌之有？不如早为之所，无使滋蔓。蔓，难图也。蔓草犹不可除，况君之宠弟乎？"（庄）公曰："多行不义必自毙，子姑待之。"

——春秋·左丘明《左传·隐公元年》

注释 Notes:

不义：违背正义。毙：死。多干坏事的人，必然自取灭亡。

不义（búyì）：injustice, immoral. 毙（bì）：to die. The person who performs too many evil acts is destined for destruction.

应用 Example sentences:

甲：这个人做尽了坏事，难道没有人管得了他吗？

乙：多行不义必自毙，他一定会遭报应的。

Ěr cáo shēn yǔ míng jù miè ,
23. 尔曹身与名俱灭，
bú fèi jiānghé wàngǔ liú .
不废江河万古流。

Your bodies and souls will fall into decay, while their fame will last as the rivers flow forever.

—translated by Xu Yuanchong

出处 Source:

王杨卢骆当时体,轻薄为文哂未休。尔曹身与名俱灭,不废江河万古流。

——唐·杜甫《戏为六绝句》之二

注释 Notes:

尔曹：你们。不废：不影响。你们这些文风浅薄的小人啊，你们的名声会随着你们的死亡消失，而被你们讥笑的那些杰出诗人的作品却像江河万古长流一样，是永远不会磨灭的。

尔曹（ěr cáo）: you (plural). 不废（bú fèi）: stay unaffected. The reputation of little men of shallow writing will disappear when they die, but the works of the great poets, even if you sneer at them, will last forever.

应用 Example sentences:

甲：现在一些别有用心的人千方百计否定英雄人物的真实存在。

乙：应该正告这些人，“尔曹身与名俱灭，不废江河万古流。”

Fāfèn wàng shí , lè yǐ wàng yōu ,
24. 发愤忘食，乐以忘忧，
bù zhī lǎo zhī jiāng zhì .
不知老之将至。

One who forgets his meals when studying hard and forgets his worries after learning something will be unaware of the approach of old age.

出处 Source:

叶公问孔丘于子路，子路不对。子曰：“女奚不曰，其为人也，发愤忘食，乐以忘忧，不知老之将至云尔。”

——春秋·孔丘《论语·述而》

注释 Notes:

（孔丘）发愤用功学习便忘记了吃饭，有所心得便高兴得忘记了忧愁，好像不知道衰老会到来一样。

This sentence was used by Confucius to describe himself: an old man who enjoys learning so much that earthly worries and the advance of old age do not bother him.

应用 Example sentences:

甲：你知道吗，我们老师每天坚持学习到深夜。

乙：这种“发愤忘食，乐以忘忧，不知老之将至”的精神值得我们学习。

Fán shì yù zé lì, bú yù zé fèi.

25. 凡事预则立，不预则废。

Preparedness ensures success; unpreparedness spells failure.

出处 Source:

凡事豫（预）则立，不豫则废。言前定，则不跲（jiá）。事前定，则不困。行前定，则不疚。道前定，则不穷。

——西汉·戴胜《礼记·中庸》

注释 Notes:

预：事先准备。废：失败。凡事有准备就能成功，否则就会失败。

预（yù）：prepare in advance. 废（fèi）：to fail.

应用 Example sentences:

甲：没有事先的计划和准备，就不能获得谈判的成功。

乙：凡事预则立，不预则废，这道理我懂。

Fùguì bù néng yín , pínjiàn bù néng yí ,

26. 富贵不能淫，贫贱不能移，

wēiwǔ bù néng qū , cǐ zhī wèi dàzhàngfu .

威武不能屈，此之谓大丈夫。

Wealth and a high position cannot corrupt him; poverty cannot sway his principles; force and power cannot make him bend. Only such a person can be called a true man.

出处 Source:

居天下之广居，立天下之正位，行天下之大道；得志，与民由之；不得志，独行其道。富贵不能淫，贫贱不能移，威武不能屈，此之谓大丈夫。

——战国·孟轲《孟子·滕文公下》

注释 Notes:

淫：惑乱。威武：武力，权势。富贵不能迷惑其内心，贫贱不能改变其志向，暴力不能使其屈服，这样的人才称得上大丈夫。

淫（yín）：to confuse. 威武（wēiwǔ）：force and power. One who adheres to principles and upholds virtues despite his circumstances is a true gentleman.

应用 Example sentences:

甲：现在有一些领导干部做不到“富贵不能淫，贫贱不能移”。

乙：他们利用职权贪污受贿，大饱私囊。

Gāo shān yǎng zhǐ ， jǐng xíng xíng zhǐ .

27. 高山仰止，景行行止。

People naturally look up to the peaks of high mountains and follow the broad path.

出处 Source:

高山仰止，景行行止。四牡騑（fēi）騑，六辔如琴。觏（gòu）尔新婚，以慰我心。

——《诗经·小雅》

注释 Notes:

仰：仰望。止：同之。景行：大道，这里比喻行为光明正大的人。比喻品德像山一样崇高的人，就会有人敬仰他；行为光明正大的人，就会有人效法他。

仰（yǎng）：look up. 止（zhǐ）：it. 景行（jǐng xíng）：main road, here refers to a righteous and straightforward person. People greatly admire those with great virtue just as they look up to the high mountains. A righteous and straightforward person will be followed by others.

应用 Example sentences:

甲：在孔庙里，“高山仰止，景行行止”的心情油然而生。

乙：是的，孔子的品德让后世的人们非常崇敬。

Gōng yù shàn qí shì, bì xiān lì qí qì.

28. 工欲善其事，必先利其器。

A craftsman must prepare his tools beforehand in order to do his work well.

出处 Source:

子曰:“工欲善其事，必先利其器。居是邦也，事其大夫之贤者，友其士之仁者。”

——春秋·孔丘《论语·卫灵公》

注释 Notes:

工匠要想做好他的工作，一定要先准备好他的工具。比喻要胜任工作，必须先学好本领。

This sentence is used metaphorically to mean one must first master working skills if one wants to be competent in a job.

应用 Example sentences:

甲：长跑训练之前，教练要求我们穿好跑鞋。

乙：“工欲善其事，必先利其器”嘛。

Gù tiān jiāng jiàng dà rèn yú shì rén yě, bì
29. 故天将降大任于是人也，必
xiān kǔ qí xīnzhì, láo qí jīngǔ, è qí
先苦其心志，劳其筋骨，饿其
tǐ fū, kōng fá qí shēn, xíng fú luàn qí suǒ
体肤，空乏其身，行拂乱其所
wéi, suǒyǐ dòng xīn rěn xìng, zēng yì qí
为，所以动心忍性，曾益其
suǒ bù néng.
所不能。

When heaven intends to bestow a great mission upon a person, it makes him suffer in mind and body, makes him endure starvation, and subjects him to poverty, difficulties and all sorts of tests to harden his willpower, toughen his temperament and increase his capabilities.

出处 Source:

孟轲曰："舜发于畎亩之中，傅说举于版筑之间，胶鬲举于鱼盐之中，管夷吾举于士，孙叔敖举于海，百里奚举于市。故天将降大任于是人也，必先苦其心志，劳其筋骨，饿其体肤，空乏其身，行拂乱其所为，所以动心忍性，曾益其所不能。"

——战国·孟轲《孟子·告子下》

注释 Notes:

心志：心意，志向。忍性：使性情坚韧。曾：同"增"。孟轲说："上天将要把重大使命赋予某人时，必先苦其心志，劳其筋骨，让他挨饿，使他穷困，让他经历磨炼，这样便可以强健他的心志，坚韧他的性情，增长他的能力。"

心志（xīnzhì）：mind and willpower. 忍性（rěn xìng）：harden one's willpower. This quote is selected from *Mencius*.

应用 Example sentences:

甲：当初他到农村劳动，常常吃不饱饭，农活又重，很多人受不了都离开了，他却坚持下来，直到后来考上大学，走上了领导岗位。

乙：这真是"天将降大任于是人也，必先苦其心志，劳其筋骨，饿其体肤"呀！

Guāngyīn sì jiàn , rìyuè rú suō .

30. 光阴似箭，日月如梭。

Time flies so quickly, like an arrow or a shuttle.

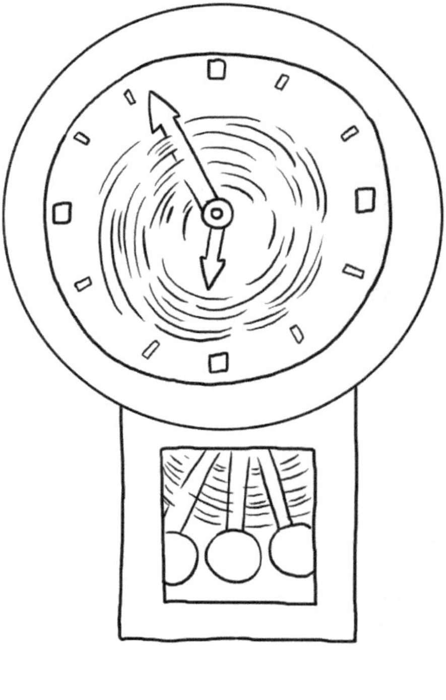

出处 Source:

但见时光流似箭。

——唐·韦庄《关河道中》

织乌，日也，往来如梭之织。

——宋·赵德麟《侯鲭录》

注释 Notes:

梭：织机上引导纬纱与经纱交织的构件。这句话多用来形容时间过得很快。

梭（suō）: shuttle of a loom.

应用 Example sentences:

甲：光阴似箭，日月如梭，转眼来中国已经三年了。

乙：是呀！我们好像还有很多东西没学呢。

Hǎi kuò píng yú yuè , tiān gāo rèn niǎo fēi .

31. 海阔凭鱼跃，天高任鸟飞。

The immense sea allows fish to jump at liberty; the vast sky allows birds to fly freely.

出处 Source:

大历末，禅僧元览题诗于竹曰："大海从鱼跃，长空任鸟飞。"

——宋·阮阅《诗话总龟》

注释 Notes:

大海辽阔，随鱼跳跃；天宇空旷，任鸟飞翔。原比喻人心胸开阔，无拘无束。现常用以比喻充分施展抱负，大显身手。

This phrase originally meant an easy and open mind. Now, it means putting one's talents to full play.

应用 Example sentences:

甲：他就任新职位后得心应手，决心大干一场。

乙："海阔凭鱼跃，天高任鸟飞"，可说是英雄有了用武之地。

Hǎi nèi cún zhījǐ, tiānyá ruò bǐlín.

32. 海内存知己，天涯若比邻。

If you have friends who know your heart, distance cannot keep you apart.

—translated by Xu Yuanchong

出处 Source:

城阙辅三秦，风烟望五津。与君离别意，同是宦游人。海内存知己，天涯若比邻。无为在岐路，儿女共沾巾。

——唐·王勃《送杜少府之任蜀州》

注释 Notes:

海内：四海之内，实指中国境内。天涯：比喻极远处。比邻：近邻。知心朋友远在天边，心里也像近邻一样感到亲切。

海内（hǎi nèi）literally means within the four seas, but actually refers to the area within China. 天涯（tiānyá）：a very far place. 比邻（bǐlín）：neighborhood.

应用 Example sentences:

甲：我们两国相隔千山万水，但彼此却亲密无间。

乙：这就叫："海内存知己，天涯若比邻"。

Hǎi shàng shēng míngyuè , tiānyá gòng cǐ shí .

33. 海上生明月，天涯共此时。

Over the sea the moon grows bright, lovers gaze upon it far, far apart.

—translated by Xu Yuanchong

出处 Source:

海上生明月，天涯共此时。情人怨遥夜，竟夕起相思。灭烛怜光满，披衣觉露滋。不堪盈手赠，还寝梦佳期。

——唐·张九龄《望月怀远》

注释 Notes:

思念我的、远在天边的情人，此时也和我一样，正望着从海上升起的一轮明月吧。

Alternative translation—My lover who is missing me from far away may be watching the moon over the sea just like me.

应用 Example sentences:

甲：每当月圆之夜，我都会情不自禁地思念起远在千里之外的亲人。

乙：难怪古人说"海上生明月，天涯共此时"，原来明月照亮思乡路呀！

Hòushēng kě wèi , yān zhī lái zhě zhī bùrú

34. 后生可畏，焉知来者之不如

jīn yě ?

今也？

The younger generation is always admirable.
Who can say they won't surpass the old?

出处 Source:

后生可畏，焉知来者之不如今也？四十、五十而无闻焉，斯亦不足畏也已。

——春秋·孔丘《论语·子罕》

注释 Notes:

后生：指后辈，年轻人。畏：敬服。这句话的意思是说，年轻人是有大作为的，谁能断定他们将来不如我们这一代人呢？

后生（hòushēng）：young people. 畏（wèi）：to admire.

应用 Example sentences:

甲：他总是看不起年轻人，说年轻人“嘴上没毛，办事不牢”。

乙：后生可畏，他不应该这样。

Huò xī , fú zhī suǒ yǐ ; fú xī , huò
35. 祸兮，福之所倚；福兮，祸
zhī suǒ fú .
之所伏。

Misfortune might be a blessing in disguise; happiness is the next-door neighbor to woes.

出处 Source:

其政闷闷，其民淳淳；其政察察，其民缺缺。祸兮，福之所倚；福兮，祸之所伏。孰知其极？

——西周·老子《道德经》

注释 Notes:

倚：依靠。伏：潜伏。灾祸里隐伏着幸福，幸福里隐藏着灾祸。

倚（yǐ）: depend on. 伏（fú）: to develop, hide in. Luck and misfortune come in turns.

应用 Example sentences:

甲：中国哲学讲祸与福同门，利与害为邻。

乙：这就是老子说的"祸兮，福之所倚；福兮，祸之所伏"。

Jǐ suǒ bú yù, wù shī yú rén.

36. 己所不欲，勿施于人。

Don't do to others what you don't want others to do to you.

出处 Source:

子贡问曰:"有一言而可以终身行之者乎?" 子曰:"其恕乎！己所不欲，勿施于人。"

——春秋·孔丘《论语·卫灵公》

注释 Notes:

欲：想要，希望。自己所不愿意接受的事情，就不要施加给别人。

欲（yù）: long for.

应用 Example sentences:

甲：我把我那个厉害的女朋友介绍给你吧?

乙：己所不欲，勿施于人。

Jiàn xián sī qí yān , jiàn bù xián ér nèi
37. 见贤思齐焉，见不贤而内
zìxǐng yě .
自省也。

On seeing a man of virtue, try to become his equal. On seeing a man of evil, try to contemplate the similar problems in yourself.

出处 Source:

见贤思齐焉，见不贤而内自省也。

——春秋·孔丘《论语·里仁》

注释 Notes:

贤：贤人，儒家称德才兼备的人为贤人。自省：亦称内省。自我反省，是儒家提倡的一种修养方法。遇见才德好的人，就应该向他看齐；遇见才德不好的人，就应该反省自己有没有和他同样的毛病。

贤（xián）: person of virtue who is both talented and virtuous according to Confucianism. 自省（zìxǐng）: to contemplate and self-reflect, a way of self-cultivation advocated by Confucianism.

应用 Example sentences:

甲："见贤思齐"是孔丘的自我修养方法之一。

乙：圣人就是圣人，难怪他说"三人行，必有我师焉"。

Jīnyù qí wài, bàixù qí zhōng.

38. 金玉其外，败絮其中。

The outside is good jade, but the inside is only cotton waste.

出处 Source:

观其坐高堂，骑大马，醉醇醴而饫肥鲜者，孰不巍巍乎可畏，赫赫乎可象也？又何往而不金玉其外，败絮其中也哉！

——明·刘基《卖柑者言》

注释 Notes:

金玉般的外表，里面全是破棉絮。比喻外表好看而实质很糟糕。

Rubbish can be coated in gold and jade. This quote is often used to describe something that is showy but useless.

应用 Example sentences:

甲：这个人徒有虚名，原来是个中看不中用的角色。

乙：这才是"金玉其外，败絮其中"呢。

Jìn xìn shū zé bùrú wú shū .

39. 尽信书则不如无书。

It is better not to believe in books at all, rather than to believe everything you read.

出处 Source:

尽信书，则不如无书。吾于武成，取二三策而已矣。仁人无敌于天下，以至仁伐至不仁，而何其血之流杵也？

——战国·孟轲《孟子·尽心下》

注释 Notes:

孟轲所说的书指《尚书》，书中有一篇讲到周武王伐纣时有“血流漂杵”的记载，孟轲很怀疑这记载的真实性。他认为以至仁伐至不仁，是不可能流那么多血的。所以他说“尽信书，则不如无书”。后来这句话转为不能完全相信书本之意，即不能死读书，要会思考。

This quote is selected from *Mencius*. The book mentioned here refers to the *Book of History*, which recorded an ancient battle where King Wu of the Zhou Dynasty (1100 BC-221 BC) overthrew King Zhou of the Shang Dynasty (1600 BC-1100 BC). The book described the war as “blood flowing so profusely that even pestles can float on it.” Mencius doubted the authenticity of the record, as he did not believe a just war would kill so many people. So he made the above comment to encourage people to think independently instead of mechanically.

应用 Example sentences:

甲：我现在才知道书上说的并不都是对的，只是代表了作者的观点罢了。

乙：所以说“尽信书则不如无书”了。

Jìn zhū zhě chì , jìn mò zhě hēi .

40. 近朱者赤，近墨者黑。

One takes the color of one's company.

出处 Source:

故近朱者赤，近墨者黑；声和则响清，形正则影直。

——晋·傅玄《太子少傅箴言》

注释 Notes:

朱：朱砂，红色颜料。靠近朱砂，会染上红色；接近墨会沾上黑色。环境的影响可以决定人的习性。现在常用来比喻接近好人，可以使人变好；接近坏人，可以使人变坏。

朱（zhū）：vermilion, a type of red pigment. The quote literally means one who comes close to vermilion will be stained red, one who touches ink shall be defiled therewith. The quote is meant to demonstrate the influence of the surrounding environment on one's character.

应用 Example sentences:

甲：年轻人比较单纯，容易“近朱者赤，近墨者黑”。

乙：所以要关心年轻人的教育，让他们少走弯路。

Jū ān sī wēi , sī zé yǒu bèi , yǒu bèi

41. 居安思危，思则有备，有备

wú huàn .

无患。

Prepare for possible dangers in a time of peace. Preparation leads to precaution and precaution averts danger.

出处 Source:

《书》曰:"居安思危。"思则有备,有备无患。敢以此规。

——春秋·左丘明《左传·襄公十一年》

注释 Notes:

居安:处于安全的境况。备:事先有准备。处安不忘危,不忘危则有准备,有准备就可防止祸患发生。

居安（jū ān）: be safe. 备（bèi）: be prepared in advance.

应用 Example sentences:

甲：和平时期有些政府官员贪污腐化、奢侈无度，国家就危险了。

乙：是的，要牢记"居安思危"。

Jūgōng jìn cuì , sǐ ér hòu yǐ .

42. 鞠躬尽瘁，死而后已。

Be bent on work and exert one's utmost until death.

出处 Source:

臣鞠躬尽力，死而后已。至于成败利钝，非臣之明所能逆睹也。

——三国·诸葛亮《后出师表》

注释 Notes:

鞠躬:弯着身子，意谓恭敬谨慎。瘁:劳累。已:停止。指不辞辛苦，勤勤恳恳，贡献出全部精神和力量，一直到死为止。

鞠躬（jūgōng）：bend one's body to show respect. 瘁（cuì）：exhaustion. 已（yǐ）：to stop.

应用 Example sentences:

甲：小李对工作是鞠躬尽瘁，死而后已。

乙：他不愧是我们学习的榜样。

Jūn zhě , zhōu yě ; shùrén zhě , shuǐ

43. 君者，舟也；庶人者，水

yě ; shuǐ zé zài zhōu , shuǐ zé fù zhōu .

也；水则载舟，水则覆舟。

The emperor is like a boat and the common people are like water. Although the water can carry the boat, it can overturn the boat as well.

出处 Source:

庶人安政，然后君子安位。传曰："君者，舟也；庶人者，水也；水则载舟，水则覆舟。"此之谓也。

——战国·荀况《荀子·王制》

注释 Notes:

载：浮托。君主是船，百姓是水。水能使船航行，也能使船翻沉。比喻民心向背决定政权存亡。

载（zài）：bear the weight of something, to support. This quote means that the will of the common people can determine the existence or destruction of a political power.

应用 Example sentences:

甲：有些领导干部当官不为百姓做事，不管百姓死活。

乙：这是他们不懂"水能载舟，亦能覆舟"的道理。

Jūnzǐ chéng rén zhī měi, bù chéng rén zhī è.

44. 君子成人之美，不成人之恶。

The gentleman helps others achieve their proper aims, but not their evil conduct.

出处 Source:

子曰："君子成人之美，不成人之恶。小人反是。"

——春秋·孔丘《论语·颜渊》

注释 Notes:

成：帮助，成全。君子乐于成全别人的好事，不促成别人的丑恶行为。后也常说"成人之美"或"成人之恶"。

成（chéng）：help to bring about. Nowadays, 成人之美 (help others to obtain something good) or 成人之恶 (help others to achieve something evil) are more often used.

应用 Example sentences:

甲：我这次出国留学多亏他从中帮忙。

乙："君子成人之美"嘛！

Jūnzǐ tǎn dàngdàng, xiǎorén cháng qīqī.
45. 君子坦荡荡，小人长戚戚。

A gentleman is always frank and poised; a petty man is usually unhappy and worried.

出处 Source:

君子坦荡荡，小人长戚戚。

——春秋·孔丘《论语·述而》

注释 Notes:

荡荡，广远。戚戚，忧虑的样子。君子心胸坦荡，通达事理，故待人接物安详而舒泰；小人心思常为物役，患得患失，故常怀戚戚之心。

荡荡（dàngdàng）：vast and far. 戚戚（qīqī）：worried. A gentleman is frank and poised because he is broad-minded. A petty man tends to be worried as he is often enslaved by material possessions.

应用 Example sentences:

甲：我最讨厌那人开会时不讲话，却总在会后嘀嘀咕咕。

乙：这就是"君子坦荡荡，小人长戚戚"。

Jūnzǐ zhī jiāo dàn rú shuǐ ,
46. 君子之交淡如水，
xiǎorén zhī jiāo gān ruò lǐ .
小人之交甘若醴。

The friendship between gentlemen appears as flavorless as water, while the friendship between petty-minded people is as sweet as rice wine.

出处 Source:

夫相收之与相弃亦远矣，且君子之交淡若水，小人之交甘若醴。君子淡以亲，小人甘以绝，彼无故以合者，则无故以离。

——战国·庄周《庄子·山木》

注释 Notes:

醴：甜酒。甘若醴，比喻一种利害相关的甜蜜亲热的感情。君子交往不用虚言，像水一样清淡；而小人相交说的都是甜言蜜语。后也单说“君子之交淡如水”。

醴（lǐ）: sweet wine. 甘若醴（gān ruò lǐ）refers to close and sweet relation involving vital interests. The friendship between gentlemen is compared to water as they do not use sweet, empty words to please the other; whereas petty-minded folks use sweet talk and flowery expressions. The first sentence is currently used more often to describe true friendship.

应用 Example sentences:

甲：咱们俩是老朋友了，你还送什么礼呀！

乙：“君子之交淡如水”我懂，这点儿东西不过是心意而已。

Lǎo dāng yì zhuàng , nìng yí bái shǒu zhī xīn ;
47. 老当益壮，宁移白首之心；
qióng qiě yì jiān , bú zhuì qīng yún zhī zhì .
穷且益坚，不坠青云之志。

Old as one is, one should still stick to one's dream. Poor as conditions are, one should refuse to give up high aspirations.

出处 Source:

冯唐易老，李广难封。屈贾谊于长沙，非无圣主；窜梁鸿于海曲，岂乏明时？所赖君子见机，达人知命。

——唐·王勃《秋日登洪府滕王阁饯别序》

注释 Notes:

老当益壮：年纪大了，志气应当更加豪壮。坠：丧失。青云之志：比喻奋起向上的气概。年纪虽老而雄心犹壮，即使头发白了也不改初衷；遭遇穷困而意志更加坚定，在任何情况下都不会丧失自己的抱负。

老当益壮（lǎo dāng yì zhuàng）: one should keep one's ambitions, even in old age. 坠（zhuì）: to lose. 青云之志（qīng yún zhī zhì）lofty aims.

应用 Example sentences:

甲：老科学家八十高龄还奋战在科研前线。

乙：真是老当益壮呀！

Lù màn màn qí xiū yuǎn xī ,
48. 路漫漫其修远兮，
wú jiāng shàng xià ér qiú suǒ .
吾将上下而求索。

The road ahead is very long. I will go up and down to seek the truth.

出处 Source:

吾令羲和弭节兮，望崦嵫而勿迫。路漫漫其修远兮，吾将上下而求索。

——战国·屈原《离骚》

注释 Notes:

漫漫：很远。修：长。求索：寻找贤人。前路漫长无尽头，我到处寻访贤人。后多用这句话形容探索正确的道路。

漫漫（màn màn）：far away. 修（xiū）：long. 求索（qiúsuǒ）：look for sages. This quote was later used to mean searching for the right path.

应用 Example sentences:

甲：他在茫茫长夜里思考着改革的前途，心里默念着“路漫漫其修远兮，吾将上下而求索”。

乙：改革的成功来之不易呀！

Lù yáo zhī mǎ lì , rì jiǔ jiàn rén xīn .

49. 路遥知马力，日久见人心。

It takes a long trip to gauge the strength of a horse and a long time to see the heart of a man.

出处 Source:

若有些好歹，我少不得报答姐姐之恩。可不道路遥知马力，日久见人心。

——《元曲选·无名氏〈争报恩〉第一折》

注释 Notes:

遥，远。路途遥远，才知道马的力气大小；相处久了，才能看出人心好坏。

遥（yáo）means far. It takes time and great effort to get to know a person.

应用 Example sentences:

甲：原来我一直把他当知心朋友，想不到他在这次商战中给我使坏。

乙："路遥知马力，日久见人心"，你以后交朋友要吸取教训了。

Mǎn zhāo sǔn , qiān shòu yì .
50. 满招损，谦受益。

One loses by pride and gains by modesty.

出处 Source:

惟德动天，无远勿届，满招损，谦受益，时乃天道。

——《尚书·大禹谟》

注释 Notes:

满：骄傲自满。招：引来。骄傲自满会招来损失，谦虚谨慎会得到教益。

满（mǎn）：conceited. 招（zhāo）：to incur.

应用 Example sentences:

甲：他一骄傲，成绩就下滑了不少。

乙：满招损，谦受益，古人说得没错！

Mǐn ér hào xué , bù chǐ xià wèn .

51. 敏而好学，不耻下问。

Be bright and fond of learning. Do not be ashamed to ask and learn from one's inferiors.

出处 Source:

子贡问曰："孔文子何以谓之文也？"子曰："敏而好学，不耻下问，是以谓之文也。"

——春秋·孔丘《论语·公冶长》

注释 Notes:

下问：向学问、地位比自己低的人请教。这句话的意思是：聪明而又好学，不以向地位、学问较低的人请教为耻辱。

下问（xià wèn）：learn from people who are less educated or in a lower position.

应用 Example sentences:

甲：他自幼"敏而好学，不耻下问"，终于成为一代大家。

乙：这就叫"少壮功夫老始成"。

Mò děngxián , báile shàonián tóu ,
52. 莫等闲，白了少年头，
kōng bēiqiè .
空悲切。

Don't linger, for the hair of the young will soon be white, and you will surely regret it.

出处 Source:

仰天长啸，壮怀激烈。三十功名尘与土，八千里路云和月。莫等闲，白了少年头，空悲切。

——宋·岳飞《满江红·写怀》

注释 Notes:

等闲：轻易地，随随便便地。不要虚度年华，不然到了满头白发之时，只有徒叹奈何了。这句话劝勉青少年不要虚度光阴，要及时努力上进。

等闲（děngxián）：easily and casually. This quote is often used to advise the young to study and work hard instead of idling away their time.

应用 Example sentences:

甲：他从小就贪玩，不好好学习，老师常劝他“莫等闲，白了少年头，空悲切”。

乙：是啊，少壮不努力，老大徒伤悲！

Qiān lǐ zhī xíng, shǐ yú zú xià.

53. 千里之行，始于足下。

A journey of a thousand miles starts with a single step.

出处 Source:

合抱之木，生于毫末；九层之台，起于累土；千里之行，始于足下。

——西周·老子《道德经》

注释 Notes:

千里远行，是从第一步开始走的。比喻学习要一步一步进取。

This quote indicates that learning should be acquired step by step.

应用 Example sentences:

甲：汉语在我面前像一座大山，我不知什么时候才能爬上去。

乙："千里之行，始于足下"，就从第一步开始吧！

Qián shì bú wàng , hòu shì zhī shī .

54. 前事不忘，后事之师。

Past experiences, not to be forgotten, are guides for the future.

出处 Source:

前事之不忘，后事之师，君若弗图，则臣力不足。

——西汉·刘向等《战国策·赵策一》

注释 Notes:

师：借鉴，教训。以前的经验教训牢记不忘，可以作为今后行事的借鉴。

师（shī）：guide or lesson.

应用 Example sentences:

甲：想起去年在大山里迷路的经历，我现在还心有余悸。

乙："前事不忘，后事之师"，今后别再到山里野游了。

Qiè ér bù shě , jīnshí kě lòu .

55. 锲而不舍，金石可镂。

With perseverance, one could carve metal and stone into shapes.

出处 Source:

骐骥一跃，不能十步；驽马十驾，功在不舍。锲而舍之，朽木不折；锲而不舍，金石可镂。

——战国·荀况《荀子·劝学》

注释 Notes:

锲：雕刻。舍：停止，放下。坚持不停止雕刻，金石也能雕成器皿。比喻办事、学习要有恒心，坚持不懈。

锲（qiè）：to carve. 舍（shě）：to stop. This quote is often used to encourage people to be persistent in their studies and work.

应用 Example sentences:

甲：汉语太难了，我根本学不会。

乙："锲而不舍，金石可镂"，只要有恒心，坚持下去你就一定能成功。

Qīng chū yú lán ér shèng yú lán .

56. 青出于蓝而胜于蓝。

Blue dye is extracted from the indigo plant, but it is bluer than the latter.

出处 Source:

学不可以已。青取于蓝，而青于蓝；冰生于水，而寒于水。

——战国·荀况《荀子·劝学》

注释 Notes:

青：五色之一。蓝：蓝草，可作染料。青色颜料从兰草中提炼出来，但颜色比蓝草更深。后以“青出于蓝而胜于蓝”比喻学生在学业成就上超过老师或后人胜过前人。

青（qīng）：indigo. 蓝（lán）：indigo plant, which is often used to obtain blue dye. The sentence is used to mean that students outdo their teachers in academic achievement, or that later generations surpass their predecessors.

应用 Example sentences:

甲：我们的老师一点儿都不保守，他希望学生在学术上超过自己，但我想没人能做到。

乙：这也不是不可能的事，没听说过“青出于蓝而胜于蓝”的话吗？

Qīngshuǐ chū fúróng , tiānrán qù diāoshì .

57. 清水出芙蓉，天然去雕饰。

Engraved by nature, the unadorned lotus flowers rise out of clear water.

出处 Source:

吴娃与越艳，窈窕夸铅红。呼来上云梯，含笑出帘栊。对客小垂手，罗衣舞春风，宾跪请休息，主人情未极。览君荆山作，江鲍堪动色。清水出芙蓉，天然去雕饰。

——唐·李白《经乱离后，天恩流夜郎，忆旧游书怀赠江夏韦太守良宰》

注释 Notes:

比喻文学作品像芙蓉出水那样自然清新。后也比喻女性的自然美丽。

This phrase was originally used to praise some literary works as being as natural and fresh as nature. Later, it was also used to compliment a woman's natural beauty.

应用 Example sentences:

甲：沈老先生的散文纯朴自然，一股清新气息扑面而来。

乙：他的诗作也是“清水出芙蓉，天然去雕饰”，和他平时说话一样。

Qióng zé dú shàn qí shēn ,
58. 穷则独善其身，
dá zé jiān jì tiānxià .
达则兼济天下。

Cultivate yourself when you are poor and powerless, and help improve the world when in power.

出处 Source:

古之人，得志，泽加于民；不得志，修身见于世。穷则独善其身，达则兼善天下。

——战国·孟轲《孟子·尽心上》

注释 Notes:

独善其身：修养好自身。善，使之善。达：得志、做官。济，有益。穷困不得志时，就把自己的德才培养好；得志做了官，就同时把天下治理好。后也说“穷则独善其身，达则兼济天下”。

独善其身（dú shàn qí shēn）：cultivate oneself. 善（shàn）：to improve. 达（dá）：have a successful career or secure an official position. 济（jì）：be beneficial.

应用 Example sentences:

甲：过去，读书人信守“穷则独善其身，达则兼济天下”的圣人教诲。

乙：这句话今天也还有现实意义。

Rénshēng zìgǔ shuí wú sǐ ,

59. 人生自古谁无死，

liú qǔ dānxīn zhào hànqīng .

留取丹心照汗青。

Who can escape death since the olden days? Let me but leave a loyal heart shining in the page of history.

出处 Source:

辛苦遭逢起一经，干戈寥落四周星。山河破碎风飘絮，身世浮沉雨打萍。惶恐滩头说惶恐，零丁洋里叹零丁。人生自古谁无死？留取丹心照汗青。

——宋·文天祥《过零丁洋》

注释 Notes:

丹心：赤诚的心。汗青：指史册。自古以来人总是要死的，但应该死得有价值，名垂青史。

丹心（dānxīn）：sincere heart. 汗青（hànqīng）：historical accounts. This famous verse is offen used to encourage people to die a worthy death.

应用 Example sentences:

甲：革命志士在生死关头往往是轻生命，重名节。

乙：这就是“人生自古谁无死，留取丹心照汗青”。

Rén shuí wú guò , guò ér néng gǎi ,
60. 人谁无过，过而能改，
shàn mò dà yān .
善莫大焉。

Everyone makes mistakes. The best thing is that you can correct them.

出处 Source:

（灵公）曰："吾知所过矣，将改之。"（士季）稽首而曰："人非圣贤，孰能无过，过而能改，善莫大焉。……君能有终，是社稷之固也。"

——战国·左丘明《左传·宣公二年》

注释 Notes:

过，指错误、过失。每个人都会犯错，犯了错以后能改正，就是最好的了。

过（guò）：mistake, error

应用 Example sentences:

甲：人不怕犯错误，只要能改正错误就是好人。

乙：对，"人谁无过，过而能改，善莫大焉。"

Sài wēng shī mǎ, yān zhī fēi fú.

61. 塞翁失马，焉知非福。

Though the old man at the border lost his horse, it might be a blessing in disguise.

出处 Source:

塞上之人有善术者，马无故亡而入胡，人皆吊之。其父曰："此何遽不为福乎？" 居数月，其马将胡骏马而归。

——西汉·刘安《淮南子·人间训》

注释 Notes:

比喻人的祸福可以相互转换，坏事可能变成好事。

This quote is used to mean that misfortune may turn into blessing and vice versa.

应用 Example sentences:

甲：唉！真倒霉，今天起晚了没赶上飞机，只能坐火车去了。

乙："塞翁失马，焉知非福"，说不定这是件好事呢。

Sān jūn kě duó shuài yě ,
62. 三军可夺帅也，
pǐfū bù kě duó zhì yě .
匹夫不可夺志也。

An army may be deprived of its commanding officer, yet a man cannot be deprived of his willpower.

出处 Source:

三军可夺帅也，匹夫不可夺志也。

——春秋·孔丘《论语·子罕》

注释 Notes:

三军：泛指军队。春秋时大国多设上、中、下三军。匹夫：古代一般指平民男子，亦泛指寻常的个人。一支军队可以丧失主帅，一个人却不可以丧失志气。

三军（sān jūn）: (literally three armies) army. During the Spring and Autumn Period (770 - 476 BC), armies in big states were divided into three types: higher army, intermediate army and lower army. 匹夫（pǐfū）: ordinary person.

应用 Example sentences:

甲：那一战几乎全军覆没，只有几个士兵誓不投降。

乙：这就是“三军可夺帅也，匹夫不可夺志也”。

Sān rén xíng bì yǒu wǒ shī yān .

63. 三人行必有我师焉。

When walking in the company of other people, there must be one I can learn from.

出处 Source:

三人行必有我师焉。择其善者而从之，其不善者而改之。

——春秋·孔丘《论语·述而》

注释 Notes:

几个人在一起，其中便一定有值得我学习的人。我选择他的优点向他学习，挑出他的缺点检查自己并加以改正。孔丘主张学无常师，无处不学。“三人”为泛指。

Confucius insists that everyone has something he can learn from and learning can happen anywhere. 三人（sān rén）literally means three people, but here it refers to several people.

应用 Example sentences:

甲：他学富五车却没有一个固定的老师，随时随地拜能者为师。

乙：他的信条就是“三人行必有我师焉”。

Shān bú zài gāo , yǒu xiān zé míng ;
64. 山不在高，有仙则名；
shuǐ bú zài shēn , yǒu lóng zé líng .
水不在深，有龙则灵。

Any mountain, high or low, can be famous with the presence of an immortal. Any river, deep or shallow, can be holy with the presence of a dragon.

出处 Source:

山不在高，有仙则名。水不在深，有龙则灵。斯是陋室，惟吾德馨。苔痕上阶绿，草色入帘青。谈笑有鸿儒，往来无白丁。可以调素琴，阅金经。无丝竹之乱耳，无案牍之劳形。南阳诸葛庐，西蜀子云亭。孔丘云：何陋之有？

——唐·刘禹锡《陋室铭》

注释 Notes:

名，著名、出名。灵，神奇。这句话后来比喻只要有名人，再普通的环境也会变得不普通。

名（míng）：famous, renowned. 灵（líng）：miraculous. This quote is a metaphor used to describe how a common place will become well-known due to the presence of a renowned figure.

应用 Example sentences:

甲：桂林山不高水不深，但桂林山水甲天下。

乙：这就是“山不在高，有仙则名；水不在深，有龙则灵”。

Shān chóng shuǐ fù yí wú lù ,
65. 山重水复疑无路，
liǔ àn huā míng yòu yì cūn .
柳暗花明又一村。

After endless mountains and rivers that have left doubt whether there is a path out, suddenly one encounters the shade of willows, bright flowers and a lovely village.

出处 Source:

莫笑农家腊酒浑，丰年留客足鸡豚。山重水复疑无路，柳暗花明又一村。箫鼓追随春社近，衣冠简朴古风存。从今若许闲乘月，拄杖无时夜叩门。

——南宋·陆游《游山西村》

注释 Notes:

山峦重重，水道弯弯，正疑无路可走；柳阴深深，花团锦簇，眼前又出现一个山村。比喻遇到困难一筹莫展的时候，解决困难的办法忽然出现在眼前。

This quote is used to indicate that a solution to a difficult situation may unexpectedly reveal itself when there seems to be no way out.

应用 Example sentences:

甲：这道数学题我怎么也解不开，他告诉我用反证法，一下子就解开了。

乙：这可是“山重水复疑无路，柳暗花明又一村”呀！

Shàozhuàng bù nǔlì, lǎodà tú shāng bēi.

66. 少壮不努力，老大徒伤悲。

One who does not work hard in youth will grieve in vain in old age.

出处 Source:

青青园中葵，朝露待日晞。阳春布德泽，万物生光辉。常恐秋节至，焜黄华叶衰。百川东到海，何时复西归。少壮不努力，老大徒伤悲。

——北宋·郭茂倩《乐府诗集·长歌行》

注释 Notes:

少壮：年轻力壮。老大：年岁大了。徒：白白地。年轻时不努力学习，上了年纪，就只有白白地悲伤而已。鼓励年轻人要及时努力学习。

少壮（shàozhuàng）：young and strong. 老大（lǎodà）：old age. 徒（tú）：in vain. This quote is often used to urge the youth to study hard.

应用 Example sentences:

甲：少年时虚度光阴，到老来一事无成，悔之晚矣！

乙：这就叫"少壮不努力，老大徒伤悲"。

Shēn wú cǎi fèng shuāng fēi yì ,
67. 身无彩凤双飞翼，
xīn yǒu língxī yì diǎn tōng .
心有灵犀一点通。

Having no wings, I can't fly to you as I please; yet, if our hearts are one, you can hear my inner call.

出处 Source:

昨夜星辰昨夜风，画楼西畔桂堂东。身无彩凤双飞翼，心有灵犀一点通。

——唐·李商隐《无题》

注释 Notes:

彩凤：有彩色羽毛的凤凰。灵犀：古代把犀牛角视为灵异之物，犀角中心的髓质像一条白线上下相通，所以说“心有灵犀一点通”。自己身上虽然没有彩凤一样的双翅，得以飞越阻隔，与心爱的人相会，但彼此的心却像灵异的犀角一样，自有一线相通。现在多比喻彼此的心思都能心领神会。

彩凤（cǎi fèng）: a colorful phoenix. 灵犀（líng xī）: mythical substance that supposedly existed in the horn of a rhino in ancient times. The substance stretched from one end to the other. The quote implies the lovers' hearts are connected. Now, it is used when people understand each other tacitly.

应用 Example sentences:

甲：想不到两位大师所用的艺术手法不约而同地一致。

乙：这就是“心有灵犀一点通”。

Shī zhī dōng yú, shōu zhī sāngyú.

68. 失之东隅，收之桑榆。

Lose at sunrise and gain at sunset.

出处 Source:

赤眉破平，士吏劳苦，始虽垂翅回溪，终能奋翼黾池，可谓失之东隅，收之桑榆。

——南朝宋·范晔《后汉书·冯异传》

注释 Notes:

东隅：东方日出处，指早晨。桑榆：指日落处，也指日暮。比喻开始有损失，最后终于取得胜利；或在这方面失败了，却在那方面获得成功。

东隅（dōng yú）refers to the morning derived from the original meaning of a place in the east where the sun rises. 桑榆（sāngyú）refers to nightfall originating from the traditional meaning of a place where the sun sets. The whole sentence means losing in the beginning and winning in the end, or failing in a certain aspect, yet succeeding in another.

应用 Example sentences:

甲：听说你又上老年大学了，真是活到老，学到老。

乙：年轻时没机会，我这也是“失之东隅，收之桑榆”。

Shí nián shù mù, bǎi nián shù rén.

69. 十年树木，百年树人。

It takes a decade to grow a forest and a century to cultivate a people.

出处 Source:

一年之计，莫如树谷；十年之计，莫如树木；终身之计，莫若树人。

——春秋·管仲《管子·权修》

注释 Notes:

树：培植，培育。培植树木需要十年，培育人才需要百年。比喻培养人才是长久之计，也指培养人才不易。后作“十年树木，百年树人”。

树（shù）：to cultivate. This quote is often used to indicate that good education is good investment for the future and is not easy.

应用 Example sentences:

甲：当今之计莫过于培养人才。

乙：“十年树木，百年树人”是至理名言。

Shì bù kěyǐ bù hóng yì, rèn zhòng ér
70. 士不可以不弘毅，任重而
dào yuǎn.
道远。

A scholar must be resolute and steadfast, for his load is heavy and the journey is long.

出处 Source:

士不可以不弘毅，任重而道远。仁以为已任，不亦重乎？死而后已，不亦远乎？

——春秋·孔丘《论语·泰伯》

注释 Notes:

士：春秋时期指读书的人，也指有志向的人。弘毅：抱负远大，意志坚强。弘毅是儒家提倡的一种美德。这句话的意思是说，读书人要刚强而有毅力，因为他们肩负重任而前程远大。

士（shì）: scholar in the Spring and Autumn Period (770 BC-476 BC), also a person with ambition. 弘毅（hóng yì）: to be ambitious and resolute, which is greatly valued in Confucianism.

应用 Example sentences:

甲：志士仁人肩负国家的命运前途，所以他们身上有一种视死如归的精神。

乙：所以说“士不可以不弘毅，任重而道远”。

Shuǐ zhì qīng zé wú yú , rén zhì chá zé

71. 水至清则无鱼，人至察则

wú tú .

无徒。

No fish can survive if the water is extremely clean. No companion can bear one whose requirements are too strict.

出处 Source:

水至清则无鱼，人至察则无徒。……举大德，赦小过，无求备于一人之义也。

——东汉·班固《汉书·东方朔传》

注释 Notes:

至清：清到极点。至察：过分精明，过分苛察。无徒：没有交往的人。水太清澈就没有鱼在里边生存，人过分精明就没有朋友。

至清（zhì qīng）：be clear to an excessive degree. 至察（zhì chá）：too harsh with details. 无徒（wú tú）：no companion.

应用 Example sentences:

甲：这人看谁都不顺眼，从不和人来往，人家也不理他。

乙：这就是"水至清则无鱼，人至察则无徒"。

Suì hán , ránhòu zhī sōngbǎi zhī hòu diāo yě .

72. 岁寒，然后知松柏之后凋也。

Only when the weather turns cold can we see that the pine and cypress leaves are the last to wither and fall.

出处 Source:

子曰："岁寒，然后知松柏之后凋也。"

——春秋·孔丘《论语·子罕》

注释 Notes:

松柏：喻栋梁之材。比喻只有经过艰苦恶劣环境的考验，才能看出一个人的高尚品质。荀况则用松柏喻君子，他说："岁不寒无以知松柏，事不难无以知君子。"

松柏（sōngbǎi）: a metaphor for people with great promise. Only in tough and harsh conditions can we find the noble quality of a man. Xun Zi once used the pine and cypress trees as a metaphor for gentlemen, "Pines and cypresses can be known only in cold weather, and gentlemen can be understood only in difficult situations."

应用 Example sentences:

甲：他是一个正直的人，逆境的艰难丝毫不能改变他的志向。

乙："岁寒，然后知松柏之后凋"，这句话正是他的写照。

Tā shān zhī shí, kě yǐ gōng yù.

73. 他山之石，可以攻玉。

Stones from other hills can serve to polish jade.

出处 Source:

鹤鸣于九皋，声闻于天。鱼在于渚，或潜在渊。乐彼之园，爰有树檀，其下维榖。他山之石，可以攻玉。

——《诗经·小雅·鹤鸣》

注释 Notes:

攻：治，加工，雕刻。别的山上的石头可以拿来打磨玉器，比喻可用别国的人才为本国效力。也比喻可以借助外力克服自身的弱点或弥补不足。

攻（gōng）: to process, to carve. This quote is extended to mean that talents from other countries could serve our country, or advice or help from others may help surmount our own shortcomings.

应用 Example sentences:

甲：美国汇聚了世界各国的优秀人才发展本国经济。

乙：他们最懂"他山之石，可以攻玉"的道理。

Tàpò tiě xié wú mì chù ,

74. 踏破铁鞋无觅处，

délái quán bú fèi gōngfu .

得来全不费工夫。

Fancy finding by sheer luck what one has searched for far and wide.

出处 Source:

老人道:“客官问别人定不知，多有人不认的他。老汉和他是邻舍……”戴宗道:“正是踏破铁鞋无觅处，得来全不费工夫。”

——元末明初·施耐庵《水浒传》第五十三回

注释 Notes:

形容花很大工夫没找到的人或物，无意中却碰上了。

This quote means that someone comes across coincidentally what he has struggled to find.

应用 Example sentences:

甲：这本书我找了好多地方都买不到，没想到在你这里见到了，太好了！

乙：这才是“踏破铁鞋无觅处，得来全不费工夫”。

Tiānshí bùrú dìlì ,
75. 天时不如地利，
dìlì bùrú rénhé .
地利不如人和。

Favorable weather is less important than advantageous terrain, and advantageous terrain is less important than unity among the people.

出处 Source:

天时不如地利，地利不如人和。三里之城，七里之郭，环而攻之而不胜。夫环而攻之，必有得天时者矣；然而不胜者，是天时不如地利也。城非不高也，池非不深也，兵革非不坚利也，米粟非不多也；委而去之，是地利不如人和也。

——战国·孟轲《孟子·公孙丑下》

注释 Notes:

天时：指天气的阴晴寒暑。地利：指高城深池、山川险阻。人和：指人心所向。在战争中，天时不及地利重要，地利不及人和重要。孟轲认为决定战争胜败的主要因素是人心向背。

天时（tiānshí）：weather. 地利（dìlì）：geographical advantages such as high city walls, deep rivers or steep mountains. 人和（rénhé）：support from the people. Mencius thought that winning a war mainly depended on support from the people.

应用 Example sentences:

甲：上甘岭战役中，天时地利都于我军不利，但最终我们的战士凭着牺牲精神取得了胜利。

乙：这就是“天时不如地利，地利不如人和”。

Tiānxià xīngwáng ， pǐfū yǒu zé .

76. 天下兴亡，匹夫有责。

Each and every person plays a part in the rise or fall of their country.

出处 Source:

是故知保天下，然后知保其国，保国者，其君其臣，肉食者谋之；保天下者，匹夫之贱，与有责焉而矣。

——清·顾炎武《日知录·正始》

注释 Notes:

天下：指国家。匹夫：古指平民百姓。国家兴亡大事，每个平民百姓都有责任。

天下（tiānxià）：country. 匹夫（pǐfū）：common people. Every man has a duty to his country.

应用 Example sentences:

甲：听说你报名参军了？

乙：对，天下兴亡，匹夫有责，我要为保卫国家贡献一份力量。

Tiān xíng jiàn , jūnzǐ yǐ zìqiáng bù xī .

77. 天行健，君子以自强不息。

As heaven moves unceasingly, gentlemen should strive constantly for self-improvement.

出处 Source:

天行健，君子以自强不息；地势坤，君子以厚德载物。

——西周·《周易·乾》

注释 Notes:

天行：天体运行，自然界运动变化。健：刚劲强健，永不停息。后多用“自强不息”形容人努力向上，不懈怠，不停息。

天行（tiān xíng）：motion of the heavenly bodies, or changes of nature. 健（jiàn）：strongly and unceasingly. Nowadays, 自强不息（zìqiáng bù xī）is used to describe the spirit of never stopping the hard work to improve oneself.

应用 Example sentences:

甲：他身残志坚，自强不息，终于完成了学业。

乙：作为健全人，我们和他比起来不由得深感惭愧。

Tiān zuò niè , yóu kě wéi ;

78. 天作孽，犹可违；

zì zuò niè , bù kě huó .

自作孽，不可活。

Man can survive natural disasters; however, they cannot run away from punishment incurred due to their evil conduct.

出处 Source:

夫人必自侮，然后人侮之；家必自毁，而后人毁之；国必自伐，而后人伐之。太甲曰："天作孽，犹可违；自作孽，不可活。"此之谓也。

——战国·孟轲《孟子·离娄上》

注释 Notes:

天灾尚可躲避，自己作孽是逃不过惩罚的。这句话是告诫人们不可以做坏事。

This quote is used to warn people not to do evil.

应用 Example sentences:

甲：他现在装可怜，以前可是威风八面，害过很多人。

乙：这就叫"天作孽，犹可违；自作孽，不可活"。

Wáng yáng ér bǔ láo , wèi wéi chí yě .

79. 亡羊而补牢，未为迟也。

It is not too late to mend the barn even after a sheep has been lost.

出处 Source:

辛庄对楚襄王曰："臣闻鄙语曰，见兔而顾犬，未为晚也；亡羊而补牢，未为迟也。"

——《战国策·楚策四》

注释 Notes:

亡：逃亡，丢失。牢：牲口圈。羊丢了，赶紧修补羊圈还不算晚。比喻出了差错后要及时补救。

亡（wáng）：to escape, to lose. 牢（láo）：barn. This quote means a mistake should be rectified in good time.

应用 Example sentences:

甲：日本侵略中国的历史，使我们懂得了国弱必受欺负的道理，所以要有强国意识。

乙：这也是"亡羊而补牢，未为迟也"。

Wǎng zhě bù kě jiàn , lái zhě yóu kě zhuī .

80. 往者不可谏，来者犹可追。

Past mistakes are beyond retrieval, but what is to come can be changed.

出处 Source:

楚狂接舆歌而过孔丘曰:“凤兮，凤兮，何德之衰?往者不可谏,来者犹可追。已而,已而,今之从政者殆而!”

——春秋·孔丘《论语·微子》

注释 Notes:

往者：过去的事。谏：规劝，使改正错误。以往的过错已无法挽回。接受教训，今后努力图新，还来得及补救。

往者(wǎng zhě): things in the past. 谏(jiàn): to admonish or persuade someone to correct their mistakes.

应用 Example sentences:

甲：过去的就让它过去吧，今后和人交往谨慎些就是了。

乙：是呀！“往者不可谏，来者犹可追”，多思无益。

Wén Wǔ zhī dào , yì zhāng yì chí .

81. 文武之道，一张一弛。

The principle of wise kings Wen and Wu was to alternate tension with relaxation.

出处 Source:

张而不弛，文武弗能也；弛而不张，文武弗为也；一张一弛，文武之道也。

——西汉·戴胜《礼记·杂记下》

注释 Notes:

文武：这里指周文王和周武王。张：紧张，拉紧弓弦。弛：松弛，放松弓弦。相传周文王和周武王处理政事像使用弓弩一样，有拉紧的时候，有放松的时候。比喻治国要宽严相济。后也比喻工作的松紧、生活的劳逸要合理安排，适当调节。

文武（Wén Wǔ）：King Wen and King Wu of the Zhou Dynasty (1046 - 771 BC). 张（zhāng）：draw the string of the bow tightly. 弛（chí）：to loosen, or unbend a bow. Legend has it that the two kings handled government affairs just like drawing a bow, sometimes tight, sometimes easy and relaxed. Later this quote is used to mean one should keep a balance in work and in life.

应用 Example sentences:

甲：前段时间太紧张了，应该放几天假让大家喘口气。

乙：应该的，“文武之道，一张一弛”，要劳逸结合嘛。

Wén dào yǒu xiān hòu ,
82. 闻道有先后，
shù yè yǒu zhuān gōng .
术业有专攻。

Some learn the truth earlier than others, and some excel in special fields.

出处 Source:

是故弟子不必不如师，师不必贤于弟子，闻道有先后，术业有专攻，如是而已。

——唐·韩愈《师说》

注释 Notes:

术业：技术本领。专攻：专门学习。接受道理有早有晚，学问和技艺上各有各的专门研究。

术业（shù yè）：skill. 专攻（zhuān gōng）：specialty.

应用 Example sentences:

甲：孔丘学无常师，有的老师还是小孩子，也受到了他的尊敬。

乙：这就叫“闻道有先后，术业有专攻”。

Wèn jūn néng yǒu jǐ duō chóu ,
83. 问君能有几多愁，
qià sì yì jiāng chūn shuǐ xiàng dōng liú .
恰似一江春水向东流。

If you ask me how much sorrow I have carried, just take a look at the spring torrent flowing endlessly eastward.

出处 Source:

春花秋月何时了，往事知多少？小楼昨夜又东风，故国不堪回首月明中。雕栏玉砌应犹在，只是朱颜改。问君能有几多愁，恰似一江春水向东流。

——南唐·李煜《虞美人》

注释 Notes:

几多：多少。问自己还有多少愁思别绪，就像一江春水向东流去，永无尽头。作者用满江春水比喻满腹的愁绪，表达了故国灭亡的悲愁悔恨。

几多（jǐ duō）: how much. The author, last emperor of the Southern Tang Dynasty (937-975), used the spring torrent to represent his profound sadness and regret for the fall of his regime.

应用 Example sentences:

甲：林黛玉是个多愁善感的人，从进贾府开始就思亲不止，泪流不尽。

乙：唉！真是“问君能有几多愁，恰似一江春水向东流”。

Wèn qú nǎ dé qīng rúxǔ ,
84. 问渠那得清如许，
wèi yǒu yuántóu huó shuǐ lái .
为有源头活水来。

How can the pool water be so clear and transparent? For fresh water comes unceasingly from the source.

出处 Source:

半亩方塘一鉴开，天光云影共徘徊。问渠那得清如许，为有源头活水来。

——宋·朱熹《观书有感》

注释 Notes:

渠：它，指池塘之水。那，通“哪”，为什么。如许：如此。池塘因为有活水源源而来，故能保持清澈。比喻学习中不断吸收新知识，故能进步不止。

渠（qú）：pool water. 那（nǎ）：why. 如许（rúxǔ）：so. This quote was extended to mean progress can be made through constantly learning new knowledge.

应用 Example sentences:

甲：昆明湖常年保持着清澈见底的水质，因为上游密云水库的清水源源不断而来。

乙：这就是“问渠那得清如许，为有源头活水来”。

Wú yù sù , wú jiàn xiǎo lì , yù sù zé

85. 无欲速，无见小利，欲速则

bù dá , jiàn xiǎo lì zé dàshì bù chéng .

不达，见小利则大事不成。

Don't make haste in handling affairs, and don't covet small gains. If you make haste, your goal may evade you; if you covet small gains, success may elude you.

出处 Source:

子夏为莒父宰，问政。子曰：“无欲速，无见小利，欲速则不达，见小利则大事不成。”

——春秋·孔丘《论语·子路》

注释 Notes:

做事不要一味图快，不要贪图小便宜。一味图快反而达不到目的，贪图小便宜办不成大事。这句话告诉人们，做事不能急功近利。

This quote is meant to tell people not to seek short-term benefits.

应用 Example sentences:

甲：办任何事情都不要一味图快，盲目赶进度。

乙：一味图快反而会“欲速则不达”。

Wú rì sān xǐng wú shēn — Wèi rén móu ér

86. 吾日三省吾身——为人谋而

bù zhōng hū ? Yǔ péngyou jiāo ér bú

不忠乎？与朋友交而不

xìn hū ? Chuán bù xí hū ?

信乎？传不习乎？

Every day I examine myself once and again: Have I tried my utmost while working for others? Have I been honest with my friends? Have I reviewed the instructions from the master diligently?

出处 Source:

曾子曰："吾日三省吾身——为人谋而不忠乎？与朋友交而不信乎？传不习乎？"

——春秋·孔丘《论语·学而》

注释 Notes:

省：自我反省，内省。传：动词作名词用，指老师的传授。曾子说：我每天都再三反省自己——为别人办事是否尽心竭力了呢？同朋友交往是否以诚相待了呢？老师教的功课是否用心学习了呢？

省（xǐng）: to self-reflect. 三省（sān xǐng）: a Confucian way of self-reflection. Zeng Zi once told his disciples to ask themselves these three questions every day in order to correct any mistakes and keep good records if none had been committed. 传（chuán）: instructor's teachings.

应用 Example sentences:

甲：他戎马一生，虽然位高权重，却不敢懈怠，坚持"吾日三省吾身"。

乙：这不是一般人能做到的。

Wù yǐ è xiǎo ér wéi zhī, wù yǐ shànxiǎo

87. 勿以恶小而为之，勿以善小

ér bù wéi.

而不为。

Don't commit any evil, no matter how insignificant it is; don't miss doing any good no matter how insignificant it is.

出处 Source:

勿以恶小而为之，勿以善小而不为。惟贤惟德，能服于人。

——《三国志·蜀志·光主传》(裴松元注)

注释 Notes:

这是刘备去世前给其子刘禅的遗诏中的话，原句为“莫以恶小而为之，莫以善小而不为。惟贤惟德，能服于人”。意为：不要认为坏事小就去做，不要以为好事不大就不去做。这句话后常用来劝人为善，恶小而为必积大恶，善小而为必积大善。

This quote is from the testamentary edict of Liu Bei (AD 161–223, founder of one of the three kingdoms) to his son Liu Chan. The original sentences were followed by another sentence saying that only virtue and morality could convince people.

应用 Example sentences:

甲：人不是生下来就成为好人、坏人的，而是不断做好事就成了好人，不断做坏事就成了坏人。

乙：所以说“勿以恶小而为之，勿以善小而不为”。

Xiān tiānxià zhī yōu ér yōu ,
88. 先天下之忧而忧，
hòu tiānxià zhī lè ér lè .
后天下之乐而乐。

Be the first to take up responsibility for the country, and the last to enjoy comfort and happiness.

出处 Source:

不以物喜，不以己悲。居庙堂之高则忧其民，处江湖之远则忧其君。是进亦忧，退亦忧。然则何时而乐耶？其必曰“先天下之忧而忧，后天下之乐而乐”乎！

——宋·范仲淹《岳阳楼记》

注释 Notes:

忧在民先，乐在民后。把国家、民族的利益放在首位，这是一种崇高的人生追求。

This famous quote demonstrates the author’s political aspirations, namely, to place national interest and the wellbeing of the people first.

应用 Example sentences:

甲：“先天下之忧而忧，后天下之乐而乐”是一种高尚的人生境界。

乙：我希望自己也能成为这样的人。

Xiǎo bù rěn , zé luàn dà móu .

89. 小不忍，则乱大谋。

Lack of patience in small matters will spoil the overall plan.

出处 Source:

巧言乱德。小不忍，则乱大谋。

——春秋·孔丘《论语·卫灵公》

注释 Notes:

小不忍：指在小事上不能忍耐。大谋：大的计划或决策。孔丘的意思是：小事上不能忍耐，就会坏了大事。

小不忍（xiǎo bù rěn）：lack of patience in small matters. 大谋（dà móu）：important plan or strategy.

应用 Example sentences:

甲：常言道“小不忍，则乱大谋”，你先不要和他们计较。

乙：我实在是忍无可忍！

Xué ér bú yàn , huì rén bú juàn .

90. 学而不厌，诲人不倦。

Study hard and never feel contented, teach the students and never feel tired.

出处 Source:

默而识之，学而不厌，诲人不倦，何有于我哉？

——春秋·孔丘《论语·述而》

注释 Notes:

厌：满足。诲：教导。努力学习而不满足，教导学生而不知疲倦。

厌（yàn）：be contented. 诲（huì）：to teach. This reflects Confucius' ideal of learning and teaching.

应用 Example sentences:

甲：谢老是一位“学而不厌，诲人不倦”的人。

乙：作为他的学生，我在他身边受益良多。

Xué ránhòu zhī bùzú , jiào ránhòu zhī kùn .

91. 学然后知不足，教然后知困。

Learning helps one realize his inadequacies, teaching helps one understand his own limitations.

出处 Source:

是故学然后知不足，教然后知困。知不足，然后能自反也；知困，然后能自强也。故曰：教学相长也。

——西汉·戴胜《礼记·学记》

注释 Notes:

通过学习，才知道自己的不足之处。通过教育学生，才发现自己学问不够。这句话说明了“教”与“学”二者之间相互促进的关系。

This quote shows teaching and learning promote and enhance each other.

应用 Example sentences:

甲：子贡初入师门，觉得自己的学问比老师还好，三年之后才知道自己远不如老师。

乙：这就是“学然后知不足”。

Yànquè ān zhī hónghú zhī zhì .

92. 燕雀安知鸿鹄之志。

How can a brambling understand the ambition of a swan?

出处 Source:

陈涉少时，尝与人佣耕，辍耕之垄上，怅恨久之，曰："苟富贵，无相忘。"佣者笑而应曰："若为佣耕，何富贵也？"陈涉叹息曰："嗟乎，燕雀安知鸿鹄之志哉！"

——西汉·司马迁《史记·陈涉世家》

注释 Notes:

燕雀：鸟名，体小，吃昆虫和植物种子。鸿鹄：天鹅。燕雀怎么能知道鸿鹄的志向呢！比喻平庸的人不能理解杰出人物的雄心壮志。

燕雀（yànquè）：brambling. 鸿鹄（hónghú）：swan. This quote is a metaphor used to mean an ordinary fellow cannot understand the mind of a great man.

应用 Example sentences:

甲：村里的人对他不顾生死进行革命宣传的行为很不理解。

乙：真是"燕雀安知鸿鹄之志"呀。

Yè jīng yú qín, huāng yú xī;
93. 业精于勤，荒于嬉；
xíng chéng yú sī, huǐ yú suí.
行成于思，毁于随。

Academic progress is achieved through diligence, but hindered by laziness. A successful deed is accomplished through thinking, but ruined by negligence.

出处 Source:

国子先生晨入太学，招诸生立馆下，诲之曰："业精于勤，荒于嬉；行成于思，毁于随。"

——唐·韩愈《进学解》

注释 Notes:

业：学业。嬉：懒散，不经心。行：实践，行为。随：马虎随便。学业靠勤勉进步，因懒散而荒废；做事成功得益于思考，马虎随便就会失败。

业（yè）：study. 嬉（xī）：sluggishness. 行（xíng）：action. 随（suí）：negligence.

应用 Example sentences:

甲：他从艺二十年，每天早上都要练功，从不荒废。

乙：业精于勤，难怪他的戏唱得这么好！

Yǒu zhì zhě shì jìng chéng .

94. 有志者事竟成。

Where there is a will, there is a way.

出处 Source:

将军前在南阳，建此大策，常以为落落难舍，有志者事竟成也。

——南朝宋·范晔《后汉书·耿弇传》

注释 Notes:

竟：终于。只要有志气，事情终会成功。

竟（jìng）：eventually.

应用 Example sentences:

甲：虽然他不是很有天赋，但通过长期的艰苦训练，他依然成为了一个出色的运动员。

乙："有志者事竟成"嘛！

Yù bù zhuó , bù chéng qì ;

95. 玉不琢，不成器；

rén bù xué , bù zhī dào .

人不学，不知道。

Just as jade without polishing will not become a useful object, a man without learning will not know the way to do things.

出处 Source:

君子如欲化民成俗，其必由学乎！玉不琢，不成器；人不学，不知道。是故古之王者，建国君民，教学为先。

——西汉·戴胜《礼记·学记》

注释 Notes:

琢：雕琢。玉石必须经玉匠把它雕成器皿才有价值。道：道理，规律。玉石不经雕琢就成不了器皿，人不经过学习就不明白道理。

琢（zhuó）: cut and polish. Jade can be made into something useful only after being cut and polished. 道（dào）: way, method.

应用 Example sentences:

甲：这孩子从小天资聪明，后来却荒废学业，一事无成。

乙：这就叫“玉不琢，不成器”。

Yù jiā zhī zuì, hé huàn wú cí.

96. 欲加之罪，何患无辞。

If you are out to condemn somebody, you can always make up a charge.

出处 Source:

不有废也，君何以兴？欲加之罪，其无辞乎？

——春秋·左丘明《左传·僖公十年》

注释 Notes:

如果想要加害于人，即使别人没有过错，也可以罗织罪名作为理由。

Alternative translation—He who has a mind to beat his dog will easily find a stick.

应用 Example sentences:

甲：秦桧以“莫须有”的罪名害死了抗金名将岳飞。

乙：真是“欲加之罪，何患无辞”。

Yù qióng qiān lǐ mù, gèng shàng yì céng lóu.

97. 欲穷千里目，更上一层楼。

You will enjoy a grander sight if you climb to a greater height.

出处 Source:

白日依山尽，黄河入海流。欲穷千里目，更上一层楼。

——唐·王之涣《登鹳雀楼》

注释 Notes:

要想看得更远，应当站得更高。比喻要想取得更大的成功，就要付出更多的努力。

This quote is a metaphor used to convey how one should work harder if he wants to become more successful.

应用 Example sentences:

甲：我登上山顶，看见大河滚滚东流，心胸豁然开朗。

乙：真是“欲穷千里目，更上一层楼”。

Céng jīng cānghǎi nán wéi shuǐ, chú què

98. 曾经沧海难为水，除却

wūshān bú shì yún.

巫山不是云。

No body of water is impressive when you have seen the sea; no cloud is beautiful, but that sea of clouds in Mount Wushan.

出处 Source:

曾经沧海难为水，除却巫山不是云。取次花丛懒回顾，半缘修道半缘君。

——唐·元稹《离思五首》之四

注释 Notes:

沧海：古人通称渤海为沧海，泛称大海。经历过沧海之后，别处的水就失去了吸引力；看过巫山美丽的云海之后，别处的云就都黯然失色了。《离思五首》是元稹写的一组悼亡诗。这两句诗体现了作者对亡妻的思念之情。

沧海（cānghǎi）：the Bohai Sea in old times, nowadays referring to the sea in general. The quote is selected from a Tang Poem in which the poet expressed his longing for his deceased wife.

应用 Example sentences:

甲：自从爱上那个姑娘之后，我就再也不想认识其他女孩儿了。

乙：你这可真是"曾经沧海难为水"呀！

Zhī jǐ zhī bǐ , bǎi zhàn bú dài .

99. 知己知彼，百战不殆。

Know yourself and know your enemy, you can fight a hundred battles without peril.

—translated by Lin Wusun

出处 Source:

知己知彼，百战不殆；不知彼而知己，一胜一负；不知彼，不知己，每战必殆。

——春秋·孙武《孙子·谋攻》

注释 Notes:

殆：危险，失败。如果对敌我双方的情况了如指掌的话，就能每战必胜。

殆（dài）：danger, failure.

应用 Example sentences:

甲：他在商战中注意搜集对手的情报，从不进行毫无准备的交易。

乙：所以他能“知己知彼，百战不殆”。

Zhī wú bù yán , yán wú bú jìn .

100. 知无不言，言无不尽。

Say all you know, and say it without reserve.

出处 Source:

知无不言，言无不尽，百人誉之不加密，百人毁之不加疏。

——宋·苏洵《衡论·远虑》

注释 Notes:

凡是知道的就说，要说就毫无保留。形容对人的态度诚恳直爽。

This quote is used to describe how people should be honest and candid with others.

应用 Example sentences:

甲：别人向他请教问题，他总是“知无不言，言无不尽”。

乙：他这个人的确很直。

Zhì zhě qiān lǜ , bì yǒu yì shī ;

101. 智者千虑，必有一失；

yú zhě qiān lǜ , bì yǒu yì dé .

愚者千虑，必有一得。

Among a thousand careful plans, a wise man may occasionally make a mistake; while a stupid person may once in a while come up with a good idea.